WINTER OLYMPIC SPORTS

ICE HOCKEY AND CURLING

by Robin Johnson

Words that are defined in the glossary are in **bold** type the first time they appear in the text.

A table of abbreviations used for the names of countries appears on page 32.

Crabtree editor: Adrianna Morganelli
Proofreader: Crystal Sikkens
Editorial director: Kathy Middleton
Production coordinator and prepress technician: Katherine Berti
Developed for Crabtree Publishing Company by RJF Publishing LLC (www.RJFpublishing.com)
Editor: Jacqueline Laks Gorman
Designer: Tammy West, Westgraphix LLC
Photo Researcher: Edward A. Thomas
Indexer: Nila Glikin

Photo Credits:
Corbis: Ints Kalnins/epa: p. 28; Wally McNamee. p. 18; Li Young/Xinhua Press: p. 29
Getty Images: front cover, p. 3, 4, 6, 7, 8, 9, 10, 14, 16, 17, 19, 26; AFP: p. 2, 12, 23, 24; Bob Thomas Sports Photography. p. 20, 22; Sports Illustrated: p. 15

Cover. Action during the 2006 gold medal ice hockey game between Sweden and Finland.

CONTENTS

Library and Archives Canada Cataloguing in Publication

Johnson, Robin (Robin R.)
Ice hockey and curling / Robin Johnson.

(Winter Olympic sports)
Includes index.
ISBN 978-0-7787-4023-0 (bound).--ISBN 978-0-7787-4042-1 (pbk.)

1. Hockey--Juvenile literature. 2. Curling--Juvenile literature. 3. Winter Olympics--Juvenile literature. I. Title. II. Series: Winter Olympic sports

GV847.25.J64 2009   j796.962   C2009-903219-8

Library of Congress Cataloging-in-Publication Data

Johnson, Robin (Robin R.)
Ice hockey and curling / Robin Johnson.
p. cm. -- (Winter Olympic sports)
Includes index.

ISBN 978-0-7787-4042-1 (pbk. : alk. paper)
-- ISBN 978-0-7787-4023-0 (reinforced library binding : alk. paper)

1. Hockey. 2. Curling. I. Title.

GV847.J65 2010
796.962--dc22

2009021495

Crabtree Publishing Company

www.crabtreebooks.com   1-800-387-7650

Published in Canada
Crabtree Publishing
616 Welland Ave.
St. Catharines, ON
L2M 5V6

Published in the United States
Crabtree Publishing
PMB16A
350 Fifth Ave., Suite 3308
New York, NY 10118

Published in the United Kingdom
Crabtree Publishing
White Cross Mills
High Town, Lancaster
LA1 4XS

Published in Australia
Crabtree Publishing
386 Mt. Alexander Rd.
Ascot Vale (Melbourne)
VIC 3032

ICE GAMES

Ice hockey and curling are team sports in which players
move small objects on icy surfaces.

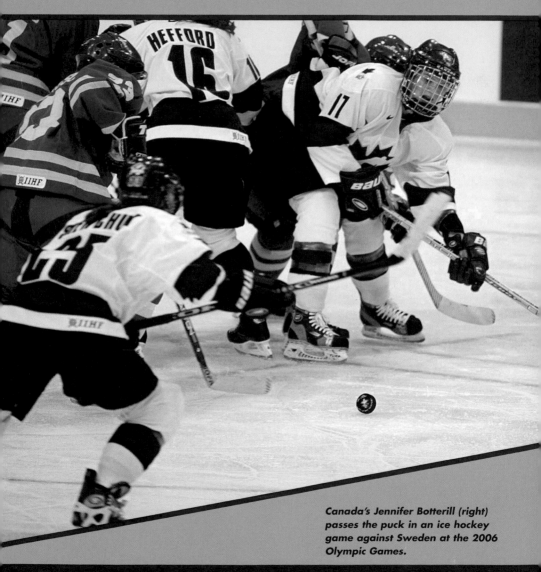

*Canada's Jennifer Botterill (right)
passes the puck in an ice hockey
game against Sweden at the 2006
Olympic Games.*

INSIDE EDGE

Curling and ice hockey are two of only four Winter Olympic sports that take place indoors. The others are figure skating and speed skating (both long track and short track).

FROZEN IN TIME

Versions of hockey and curling have been played on frozen ponds for hundreds of years. The first organized hockey tournament took place at McGill University in Montreal, Canada, in 1879. The first known curling competition was held in Paisley, Scotland, in 1541. Both sports have long histories in the Olympic Games.

FAST AND SLOW

Ice hockey and curling may have some similarities, but there are differences as well. Ice hockey is a high-speed game with constant movement and action. In contrast, curling is more a game of strategy, thought, and patience.

Oliver Axnick (GER) takes careful aim in a 2006 Olympic curling match.

- The Olympic Games were first held in Olympia, in ancient Greece, around 3,000 years ago. They took place every four years until they were abolished in 393 A.D. A Frenchman named Pierre Coubertin (1863–1937) revived the Games, and the first modern Olympics—which featured only summer sports—were held in Athens in 1896.

- The first Olympic Winter Games were held in 1924 in Chamonix, France. The Winter Games were then held every four years except in 1940 and 1944 (because of World War II), taking place in the same year as the Summer Games, until 1992.

- The International Olympic Committee decided to stage the Summer and Winter Games in different years, so there was only a two-year gap before the next Winter Games were held in 1994. They have been held every four years from that time.

- The symbol of the Olympic Games is five interlocking colored rings. Together, they represent the union of the five regions of the world—Africa, the Americas, Asia, Europe, and Oceania (Australia and the Pacific Islands)—as athletes come together to compete in the Games.

ICE HOCKEY: THE BASICS

Alexander Kharitonov (RUS) scores a goal against Kazakhstan at the 2006 Games.

In ice hockey games, players use long, narrow sticks to shoot pucks into the opposing team's net. The team with the most goals after three 20-minute periods wins the game.

ORIGINS OF THE GAME

Ice hockey began hundreds of years ago in Europe, perhaps as early as the 1500s. The British brought the sport to North America, where soldiers in Nova Scotia, Canada, played early games. In 1879, college students at McGill University in Montreal held competitions and developed the first known set of hockey rules. In the next few years, ice hockey made its way to the United States.

OLYMPIC HISTORY

Ice hockey was first played at the Olympics in 1920, but at that time it was part of the Summer Games! The sport moved to the Winter Olympics in 1924 and has been there since that time.

THINKING INSIDE THE BOX

Players get penalties for breaking the rules in an ice hockey game. When penalties are called—for actions like tripping, slashing, spearing, and hooking—players must spend time in an off-ice area called the penalty box.

A NUMBERS GAME

There are about 20 players on an Olympic hockey team, but teams can have no more than six players on the ice at one time. At the 2010 Games, 12 men's teams and eight women's teams will face off in separate **round robin** tournaments.

DID YOU KNOW?

• *The word hockey comes from the French word* hocquet, *which means "stick."*

• *Long ago, Canadians called ice hockey "shinty."*

• *Ice hockey is the only Olympic sport in which a puck is used.*

• *The sides of hockey nets— called goal posts—are always painted red.*

SIZE MATTERS

Olympic ice hockey has traditionally been played on international rinks, which measure 200 feet x 98.5 feet (61 m x 30 m). At the Vancouver 2010 Olympics, however, standard North American rinks—which are 13 feet (four m) narrower—will be used for the first time. Ice hockey will take place at Canada Hockey Place and the UBC Thunderbird Arena. Using existing rinks there will save millions of dollars in construction costs.

LEARN THE LINGO

Overtime—extra time added to a hockey game if the score is tied after **regulation** play
Period—a section of time in a hockey game
Puck—a hard, rubber disk used in ice hockey
Rink—the ice surface on which hockey games are played

LET'S OUT, THEY SCORE!

There are three forwards on an ice hockey team: center, right wing, and left wing. Forwards move the puck toward their opponent's net and try to score goals.

A skirmish among forwards—
Finland's Petra Vaarakallio (left)
and Katie King (USA)—in 2002.

glove

hockey
stick

pad

skate

puck

Hockey pucks can move fast—at speeds of more than 93 MPH (150 km/h)! The hockey puck used in the Olympics is one inch (2.54 cm) thick and three inches (7.62 cm) in diameter. It must weigh between 5.5 and six pounds (156 and 170 gm).

GEAR UP

Hockey forwards wear ice skates, helmets, gloves, and thick, protective pads under their uniforms. They use narrow sticks made of wood or other hard materials to pass and shoot the puck.

SLAP HAPPY

There are a lot of shots in ice hockey, including wrist shots, snap shots, and slap shots. Slap shots—the fastest hockey shots—can reach speeds of more than 100 MPH (161 km/h)!

HATS OFF TO YOU

The term "hat trick" was first used in Guelph, Canada, in the 1950s. When home-team players scored three goals in a single game, a local hat company gave them new hats! Now fans throw their own hats onto the ice to celebrate hat tricks.

HAYLEY'S A COMET

Forward Hayley Wickenheiser led the Canadian women's ice hockey team to Olympic gold in 2002 and 2006. At the 2002 Games, she scored seven goals, helping her teammates win all five games and outscore their opponents 35–5!

Pavel Bure (RUS) in action in 2002.

LEARN THE LINGO

Assist—to pass the puck to a player who scores

Face-off—when a **referee** drops the puck between two opposing players to begin or resume play

Hat trick—when a player scores three goals in a game

THE RUSSIAN ROCKET

Right-winger Pavel Bure (RUS) skated to the **podium** in two Olympic Games. In 1998—when Russia won the silver medal—he led the men's ice hockey tournament with nine goals, scoring five in the semifinal match. In 2002, Bure played in all of Russia's games and helped his team win the bronze medal—even though he had broken his hand just weeks before the Games!

ON THE DEFENSIVE

There are three defensive positions in ice hockey games: right defense, left defense, and goaltender (or goalie). The defense players try to keep the puck away from their net. The goalie guards the net and tries to prevent the other team from scoring.

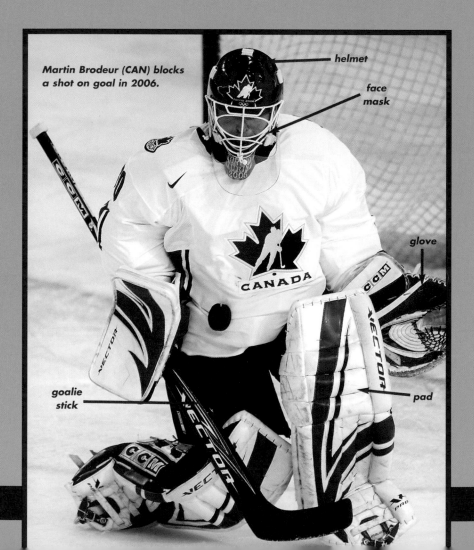

Martin Brodeur (CAN) blocks a shot on goal in 2006.

helmet

face mask

glove

goalie stick

pad

CANADA

SUPER STATS

Goalie Antero Niittymäki (FIN)—the **MVP** of the 2006 men's hockey tournament at the Olympics—posted three shutouts in six games and allowed an average of only 1.34 goals per game.

GEAR UP

Right and left defense players use the same equipment as forwards. Goalies wear helmets with full face masks, thick pads to protect their legs, and gloves to catch or block shots. They use sticks with wide blades to help stop goals.

Switzerland's Sandrine Ray (right) controls the puck against the defense of Russia's Elena Byalkovskaya.

CAPTAIN CHRIS

Defenseman Chris Chelios (USA) captained his country's men's ice hockey team from 1998 through 2006, battling to a silver-medal finish at the 2002 Games. That year, Canada won the gold.

A MAN(ON)'S WORLD

Goaltender Manon Rhéaume (CAN) helped her team skate to the silver spot in the women's tournament in 1998. Rhéaume was the first woman to play in the **National Hockey League** (NHL), in an exhibition game in 1992.

PROTECTING THEIR ASSETS

The first **professional** hockey players wore only thick sweaters and gloves for protection. Goaltenders began wearing masks in 1959. Today, goalies wear about 40 pounds (18 kg) of protective gear!

LEARN THE LINGO

Clearing the puck—getting the puck out of the defensive end
Pulling the goalie—taking the goalie off the ice for a short time and replacing him or her with an extra skater to get a chance to score
Shutout—when the goalie stops all the shots in a game

YES, HE CAN!

Goalie Martin Brodeur (CAN) helped his team skate their way to gold at the 2002 Olympics. Brodeur—who guarded the net in every game of the series but one—stopped 31 out of 33 shots in the gold-medal match against the United States.

MEN'S ICE HOCKEY: 1920–1952

Only **amateur** ice hockey players could represent their countries in early Olympic competitions. Professional hockey players—including those in the NHL—were not allowed to compete.

Canada vs. the United States, playing outdoors in 1924.

CANADA'S GOLDEN YEARS

Canada dominated Olympic ice hockey in the early years of the sport, winning six out of the first seven gold medals. In 1936, Canada lost the tournament to Great Britain. It was the last medal that Great Britain ever won in Olympic ice hockey.

IN THE BEGINNING

At the first Olympic ice hockey tournament, there were two 20-minute periods of play, with seven men on the ice for each team. The extra player—called a rover—moved around the rink and helped his team as needed. That first tournament, in 1920, was played in an indoor rink, but the 1924 competition was held outdoors.

SHORT NOTICE

Canada's victorious 1920 team needed some help before the Games. When the invitation to enter the Olympics—to be played in Belgium—came, the team was away from home, playing in a tournament. They did not have enough time to return home before getting on the boat to go overseas. Money had to be raised to buy them the clothes they needed.

CANADIAN MOOSE

Harry "Moose" Watson (CAN) scored 37 goals in the 1924 hockey tournament—an Olympic record that remains unbroken. In the final game of the series, Watson was knocked out cold. He recovered from his injury and wound up scoring two goals! Canada beat the United States for the gold. Great Britain won the bronze medal.

DID YOU KNOW?

• At the 1924 Games, Canada outscored its opponents 110–3!

• In 1928, Canada's hockey team was so good that it was advanced to the final round, where the players shutout their opponents and won the gold medal.

• In 1948, the United States was **disqualified** from the Olympic ice hockey tournament for entering two teams into competition.

ROUGHHOUSING

Three U.S. players in the 1952 tournament played so roughly that they spent more time in the penalty box than all of the players on the other teams.

WHAT'S THE DIFFERENCE?

At the 1948 Games, Canada tied Czechoslovakia for first place in the men's ice hockey tournament. Each team won seven games and tied when they faced each other. Canada was awarded the gold medal based on **goal difference**.

MEN'S ICE HOCKEY: 1956–1994

Men's Olympic ice hockey saw a shift from Canadian domination to Soviet supremacy.

Peter Forsberg (SWE) scores the winning goal during the dramatic shootout *against Canada in 1994.*

The Soviet team that won the gold medal in 1956 was extremely powerful. The team did not lose a single game, finishing with a perfect record of 7–0! The Soviets also outscored their opponents 40 goals to nine!

• Australia has sent only one ice hockey team to the Olympic Games. The team competed in 1960 and finished "down under" all the other teams.

• Canada did not send an ice hockey team to the 1972 or 1976 Games because their best players — who were professionals — were not allowed to compete.

• In 1992, six nations from the former Soviet Union competed together — and won gold — as the "Unified Team."

SOVIET SUPER POWERS

In 1956, the Soviet Union began competing in the Olympic Games. They dominated men's ice hockey for more than 30 years, winning all but two gold medals from their **debut** through 1988. The United States won the tournament in 1960 and 1980.

PROS AND CONS

In 1986, the International Olympic Committee voted to let professional ice hockey players take part in the Games. The NHL did not want to interrupt its regular hockey schedule, however, and did not allow its players to compete.

NOT TOO VLAD

Goaltender Vladislav Tretiak (URS) helped his team skate away with three golds and one silver medal from 1972 through 1984. Tretiak — who never played in the NHL — was named to the Hockey Hall of Fame in 1989. He was the first player born and trained in the Soviet Union ever selected for the Hall of Fame.

HOW SWEDE IT IS

In the 1994 ice hockey finals, Sweden and Canada faced off in the first shootout ever held in Olympic competition. Peter Forsberg — the final shooter for Sweden — faked a forehand shot and then slipped a one-handed backhand shot into the net, earning his country its first gold medal in the sport.

SAVED FROM TRAGEDY

In 1950, the Soviet national hockey team was involved in a plane crash that claimed the lives of almost the entire team. One team member, Vsevolod Bobrov, survived because he overslept and missed the plane and took the train instead. Bobrov was a member of the team that won Olympic gold in 1956. He even led the team in scoring, with nine goals and two assists.

MEN'S ICE HOCKEY: 1998–2006

In 1998, the NHL suspended its games for two weeks to allow players to compete in the Olympics. Some of the greatest NHL players have represented their home countries at the Games ever since.

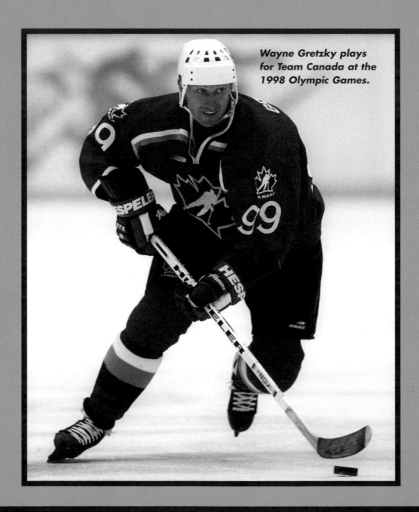

Wayne Gretzky plays for Team Canada at the 1998 Olympic Games.

2006 OLYMPIC MEDALISTS: GOLD: SWEDEN

SUPER STATS

Canada and the Soviet Union share the record for the most golds in men's Olympic ice hockey, with seven medals each. The United States and Sweden have each won the event twice, while Great Britain, the Czech Republic, and the Unified Team have one gold apiece.

BACK ON TOP

In 2002, the Canadian men's ice hockey team won its first Olympic gold medal in 50 years, defeating the United States. Captain Mario Lemieux led the team to victory, while forward Joe Sakic—who scored the medal-winning goal—was named tournament MVP. Sakic had four goals and six assists in the tournament.

LUCKY LOONIE LEGEND

A Canadian ice-maker buried a one-dollar coin (called a loonie) under the ice at the 2002 Games. The loonie proved lucky for Canada when both its men's and women's ice hockey teams won gold medals!

THE GREAT ONE

Wayne Gretzky (CAN) is considered by most to be the best hockey player of all time. He never won a medal in Olympic ice hockey, however. Gretzky competed in the 1998 Olympics, but his team fell just short of the podium with a fourth-place finish. Gretzky could claim a piece of gold in 2002, though. As executive director of Team Canada that year, he put together the Canadian team that won the gold medal.

NICK OF TIME

In the 2006 gold-medal game, Nicklas Lidström's rock-solid defense and game-winning goal—10 seconds into the final period of play—helped Sweden edge out Finland by a score of 3–2. It was the first all-**Scandinavian** final in Olympic ice hockey history.

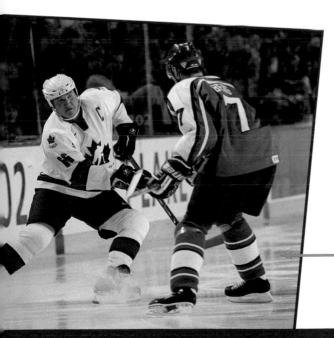

Canada's Mario Lemieux (left) in action in 2002.

WOMEN'S ICE HOCKEY

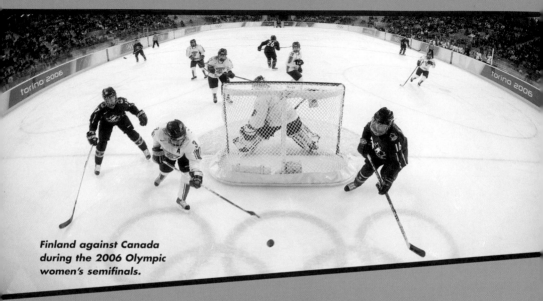

Finland against Canada during the 2006 Olympic women's semifinals.

Women's ice hockey debuted at the 1998 Winter Olympics. Teams from Canada and the United States have dominated the competition so far.

WOMEN vs. MEN

Women's Olympic ice hockey follows the same rules as the men's event, with two important differences—all women must wear helmets with full face masks, and **body checking** is not allowed.

IN HER BLOOD

Forward Jennifer Botterill (CAN) competed in all three women's Olympic ice hockey tournaments, skating away with two golds and one silver in the event. Botterill has ice in her blood—her mother was a two-time Olympic speed skater and her brother played in the NHL.

In the 2006 women's ice hockey tournament, Canada outscored its opponents 46 goals to two!

ROOTH FOR SWEDEN

Forward Maria Rooth (SWE) helped her team reach the podium at the 2002 and 2006 Olympics. In 2006, she led her team to a silver medal, earning five goals — including the game-winning goal in a semifinal shootout — and four assists in the series.

Cammi Granato (USA) celebrates her team's gold medal win in 1998.

DOUBLE DUTY

Hayley Wickenheiser (CAN) played more than ice hockey for her country. She also represented Canada in the 2000 Summer Olympics, in softball. Among her other feats was her play with Finland's Kirkkonummi Salamat hockey team. With that team, in January 2003, she became the first woman to score a goal in a men's professional hockey league.

DRESSED FOR SUCCESS?

Women in the early 1900s had to wear ankle-length skirts when they played the sport of ice hockey!

OLYMPIC MEDALS IN WOMEN'S ICE HOCKEY

Only four countries have won medals in the relatively young history of Olympic women's ice hockey.

Rank	Country	Gold	Silver	Bronze	Total Medals
1	Canada	2	1	0	3
2	United States	1	1	1	3
3	Sweden	0	1	1	2
4	Finland	0	0	1	1

MIRACLES
ON ICE

Dominik Hašek (CZE) defends the net against Canada in the dramatic 1998 semifinal game.

Dramatic comebacks and surprising upsets make ice hockey games some of the most memorable events in Winter Olympic history.

DO YOU BELIEVE IN MIRACLES?

In 1980, the U.S. men's hockey team—made up of amateur college players—faced the Soviet Union in the Olympic semifinal match. By the middle of the third period, the score was tied, 3–3. With 10 minutes left in the game, Mike Eruzione (USA) scored the game-winning goal. The United States went on to defeat Finland in the finals and capture the gold. Since then, the win over the Soviets has been called the "Miracle on Ice."

CZECH IT OUT!

The 1998 semifinal game between Canada and the Czech Republic is considered one of the greatest displays of goaltending in Olympic history. Goalie Dominik "The Dominator" Hašek (CZE) stopped all but one of Canada's shots in regulation play. When the tie game went to a shootout, he continued to dominate the net, stopping all five of Canada's shots. Hašek went on to shutout Russia for the gold medal.

THE GOAL HEARD AROUND THE WORLD

In 1972, a historic ice hockey event took place outside Olympic competition. The Summit Series was an eight-game tournament between Canada and the Soviet Union in which the best players from both countries faced off for the first time. After tying one game and winning three apiece, the teams were even going into the final game. Both teams battled hard, each racking up five goals. With just 34 seconds left in the game, Paul Henderson scored the winning goal for Canada.

DID YOU KNOW?

The United States won the first Olympic gold medal ever awarded in women's ice hockey in 1998, but Canada was heavily favored to win the tournament. The U.S. team was led by its captain, Catherine "Cammi" Granato. In 2008, she became the first woman inducted into the U.S. Hockey Hall of Fame.

UPSET ON ICE

At the 2006 Olympics, Sweden's women's hockey team defeated the heavily favored U.S. team 3–2 in a dramatic shootout in the semifinal round. When Sweden battled Canada in the finals, it was the first gold-medal match in women's international competition in which Canada and the United States did not face off.

Mike Eruzione (center) of Team USA in action against the Soviet Union, 1980.

The U.S. men in their bronze medal match with Great Britain in 2006.

CURLING: THE BASICS

Curling is often called "chess on ice." It is a game of strategy in which players maneuver their pieces into winning positions.

A PERFECT 10

At the 2010 Olympics, ten men's curling teams and ten women's curling teams will face off in separate round robin tournaments. All events will be held at Vancouver Olympic Centre.

LEARN THE LINGO

Bonspiel—a curling tournament
End—one round in a curling game
Rink—a curling team and the building in which the team plays
Stones—heavy, round playing pieces with handles; also called rocks
Throw—to slide a stone along the ice

CURLING 101

In curling bonspiels, two teams take turns sliding heavy polished stones toward circular rings painted on the ice. Curlers sweep the ice in front of the stones to direct them and control their speed. Teams earn points by throwing stones closest to the center of the rings. Only one team scores in each end. The team with the most points after ten ends wins the game.

THE CREW

There are four players on a curling rink. Each player throws two rocks per end. A player called the *lead* throws first, a player called the *second* throws next, and a player called the *vice* throws third. The *skip*—who is the captain of the team—makes strategy decisions, shouts instructions to the other players, and almost always throws the crucial last stones in each end.

CURLING ROCKS!

In the early days of curling, players threw flat-bottomed rocks that were found on riverbeds. They competed on frozen lakes and ponds.

IN THE HOUSE

Olympic curling tournaments take place indoors on refrigerated sheets of ice. The sheets are 138 feet (42 m) long and 14 feet (4 m) wide, with targets on both ends.

house

button

broom

stone

A player waits for the stone in the curling house.

HOUSE SWEET HOUSE

Curlers throw stones toward a target area called the *house*. The house consists of four **concentric** circles. The outside circle is 12 feet (3.7 m) in diameter, while the innermost circle—called the *button*—is only one foot (0.3 m) in diameter. Curlers aim for the button and try to knock the other team's stones out of the house.

A CLEAN SWEEP

Curlers use specially made **synthetic** push brooms to quickly sweep the area around moving stones. Curlers once used straw brooms in competition, but they left bits of straw on the ice! Brooms are used because sweeping melts the ice a bit, which reduces the friction between the ice surface and the stones. Then, the stones can travel farther on the ice.

SUIT UP

Curlers wear warm, loose-fitting clothing and a different type of shoe on each foot. The slider shoe has a slippery sole that lets the curler glide along the ice. The gripper shoe has a nonslip sole that allows the curler to stand and balance during the game.

NICE ICE

Water droplets are sprinkled on the ice before bonspiels. The droplets freeze into tiny bumps—called *pebbled ice*—that help stones grip the surface and allow curlers to control their shots.

LEARN THE LINGO

Blank end—an end in which no points are scored
Hack—footholds on the ice from which curlers push off and throw their stones
Hog line—the line behind which curlers must release their stones
Wide—a stone that slides outside the sheet's boundary lines

Skip Anette Norberg (SWE) releases the stone in the women's final in 2006.

MEN'S CURLING

Men's curling debuted at the first Winter Games in 1924. It returned as a demonstration sport in 1932, 1988, and 1992, before becoming an official Olympic event in 1998.

Peja Lindholm, Sweden's skip, shouts after delivering a stone during his team's semifinal against Canada in 2002.

Four countries have curled their way to Olympic glory in the men's event: Great Britain (1924), Switzerland (1998), Norway (2002), and Canada (2006).

MEDALS FOR EVERYONE!

The 1924 men's curling competition was held outdoors. Only three countries took part in the tournament—Great Britain, Sweden, and France—but there were two Swedish teams. The competition was not recognized as an official Olympic event until 2006. Medals were awarded **retroactively** at that time.

SKIP'S CHOICE

Although the skip almost always throws the last stones in the end, the rules do not say that he has to. Some skips prefer to throw second or third.

THE ROARING GAME

Curling is known as "the roaring game." The heavy curling stones make loud roaring sounds as they slide down the ice. Skips also roar at their teams to sweep harder or stop sweeping as the stones approach the house.

DID YOU KNOW?

• At the 2002 Olympics, the men's gold-medal game was decided in the final throw! In a dramatic upset, Norway edged out the favored Canadian team and won by a score of 6–5.

• When skip Brad Gushue (CAN) led his rink to Olympic gold in 2006, it was the first major senior-level event in which he had ever competed! Amazingly, Gushue was only 25 years old.

LEARN THE LINGO

Curl—the curve of a stone as it moves down the ice
Hurry—the command from the skip to sweep
Whoa—the command from the skip to stop sweeping

HALL OF FAME

Both Canada and the United States have Curling Halls of Fame. The Canadian hall inducted its first members in 1973. The U.S. hall inducted its first members in 1984.

NEW FANS IN ITALY

When the 2006 Olympics began in Turin, Italy, curling wasn't exactly a popular sport in the nation. Italy, however, got to enter a team in the competition because it was the host country. Millions of Italians watched the competiton on television and were fascinated by the sport. They were also captivated by Jöel Retornaz, the 22-year-old skip of the Italian team. The Italian men did score upset wins over Canada and the United States, but they wound up in seventh place.

WOMEN'S CURLING

Canada's Sandra Schmirler in action at the 1998 Games.

Women's curling was a demonstration sport at the 1988 and 1992 Games. It debuted as an official Olympic event in 1998.

Three countries have curled their way to victory in the women's Olympic event: Canada (1998), Great Britain (2002), and Sweden (2006).

HAMMER TIME

The hammer is the last—and most important—stone thrown in each end. The hammer often determines which team gets points in that round of play. The team that does not score gets the hammer in the next end.

OLDER AND WISER

Olympic curlers are often older than other Olympic athletes. The sport is a mental game that requires extreme focus and nerves of steel—traits that usually come with experience and many years of practice and training.

STARTING YOUNG

Erika Brown (USA) was a member of the 1988 U.S. women's curling team—when curling was a demonstration sport—at just 15 years old! Her father began teaching her how to curl when she was seven. Since she was too small to handle the stones, she used tissue boxes and ashtrays instead!

CHAMPIONS OF THE WORLD

World Championships in curling for men have been held since 1959. World Championships for women began 20 years later, in 1979. Scotland dominated the first years of men's competition, with five straight wins from 1959 to 1963. Scotland also won the first three years of women's competition, with victories in 1979, 1980, and 1981.

SCHMIRLER THE CURLER

Skip Sandra Schmirler (CAN) led her team to gold in the first official Olympic women's curling event in 1998. In her last shot of the semifinal game—which was tied at five points apiece—Schmirler inched inside her opponent's closest stone and sent Canada to the finals. There, she and her team held on to an early lead against Denmark to win the gold. Sadly, "Schmirler the Curler" died in 2000 at just 36 years old.

WE GIVE UP!

A curling team can **concede** a game before it is finished if the skip feels the team is too far behind to catch up. At the Olympics, teams must complete eight ends before they stop throwing stones and throw in the towel.

MIXING IT UP

Shannon Kleibrink (CAN), the skip of Canada's bronze medal winning women's team in 2006, was the first woman to win the Canadian **Mixed** Curling Championship as skip. The teams were made up of both men and women.

A SNAPSHOT OF THE VANCOUVER 2010 WINTER OLYMPICS

ICE HOCKEY AND CURLING
THE ATHLETES

Everyone is getting ready for Vancouver in 2010! Olympic teams are still being determined. The listings below include the top teams in the most recent World and Olympic championships. Who among them will be the athletes to watch in the Vancouver Winter Olympics? Visit the Web site www.vancouver2010.com for more information about the upcoming competitions.

ICE HOCKEY

IIHF World Championship

Men 2009:
1. Russia
2. Canada
3. Sweden

Men 2008:
1. Russia
2. Canada
3. Finland

Men 2007:
1. Canada
2. Finland
3. Russia

Women 2009:
1. USA
2. Canada
3. Finland

Women 2008:
1. USA
2. Canada
3. Finland

Women 2007:
1. Canada
2. USA
3. Sweden

Olympics

Men 2006:
1. Sweden
2. Finland
3. Czech Republic

Men 2002:
1. Canada
2. USA
3. Russia

Men 1998:
1. Czech Republic
2. Russia
3. Finland

Women 2006:
1. Canada
2. Sweden
3. USA

Women 2002:
1. Canada
2. USA
3. Sweden

Women 1998:
1. USA
2. Canada
3. Finland

Canadian Sidney Crosby fights for the puck with Denmark's Daniel Nielsen during their IIHF World Championship ice hockey preliminary Group D match in the Skonto Hall in Riga, Latvia May 5, 2006.

CURLING

World Curling Federation standings

Men 2009:
1. Scotland
2. Canada
3. Norway

Men 2008:
1. Canada
2. Scotland
3. Norway

Men 2007:
1. Canada
2. Germany
3. USA

Women 2009:
1. China
2. Sweden
3. Denmark

Women 2008:
1. Canada
2. China
3. Switzerland

Women 2007:
1. Canada
2. Denmark
3. Scotland/GBR

Olympics

Men 2006:
1. Canada
2. Finland
3. USA

Men 2002:
1. Norway
2. Canada
3. Switzerland

Men 1998:
1. Switzerland
2. Canada
3. Norway

Women 2006:
1. Sweden
2. Switzerland
3. Canada

Women 2002:
1. Great Britain
2. Switzerland
3. Canada

Women 1998:
1. Canada
2. Denmark
3. Sweden

China defeats Canada 6-5 in the women's curling final to win the 24th World Winter Universiade at Harbin, Heilongjiang Province, China in February of 2009.

THE VENUES IN VANCOUVER

HOCKEY: CANADA HOCKEY PLACE

- *venue capacity: 18,630*
- *located in Vancouver, British Columbia*
- *elevation: 26 feet (8 m)*

UBC THUNDERBIRD ARENA

- *venue capacity: 7,200*
- *located on the campus of University of British Columbia in Vancouver, British Columbia*
- *elevation: 295 (90 m)*

CURLING: VANCOUVER OLYMPIC/ PARALYMPIC CENTRE

- *venue capacity: 6,000*
- *located in Vancouver, British Columbia*
- *elevation: 242 feet (74 m)*

GLOSSARY

amateur An athlete who is not paid to play his or her sport

body checking To knock against an opponent with part of the body in ice hockey

concede To admit defeat and allow the other team to win

concentric A series of circles around a center point

debut To perform something for the first time or the first time an event is added to competition

demonstration sport A sport that is played at the Olympics on a trial basis

disqualified To be eliminated from competition for not following the rules

goal difference The number of goals scored minus the number of goals allowed

granite A hard, tough rock

MVP Most Valuable Player, an award given to the person who helped his or her team the most during a game or tournament

mixed Consisting of both men and women

National Hockey League (NHL) A professional hockey league whose teams are based in Canada and the United States

podium A platform on which the winners of an event stand

professional An athlete who is paid to play his or her sport

referee The person who starts and stops play and calls penalties in an ice hockey game

regulation The standard three periods of play in a hockey game

retroactively Applying to or done after events have taken place

round robin A tournament in which each team plays every other team

Scandinavian Referring to several northern European countries including Norway, Denmark, Sweden, Iceland, and Finland

shootout Taking turns shooting on the net in order to break a tie

synthetic Made from materials that are not natural

FIND OUT MORE

BOOKS

Campbell, Cassie, and Lorna Schultz Nicholson. *H.E.A.R.T.* (Bolton, Ontario: Fenn Publishing, 2007)

Crossingham, John. *Slap Shot Hockey* (St. Catharines, Ontario: Crabtree Publishing, 2008)

Jones, Colleen. *Curling Secrets: How to Think and Play Like a Pro* (Halifax, Nova Scotia: Nimbus Publishing, 2007)

Thomas, Keltie. *How Hockey Works* (Toronto: Maple Tree Press, 2006)

Weeks, Bob. *Curling for Dummies, 2nd ed.* (Mississauga, Ontario: John Wiley & Sons Canada, 2006)

Zweig, Eric. *Long Shot: How the Winnipeg Falcons Won the First Olympic Hockey Gold* (Halifax, Nova Scotia: James Lorimer & Company, 2007)

WEB SITES

Canadian Curling Association   **www.curling.ca**
The official site of the Canadian governing body of curling

Hockey Canada   **www.hockeycanada.ca**
The official site of the Canadian governing body of ice hockey

International Ice Hockey Federation (IIHF)   **www.iihf.com**
The official site of the international governing body of ice hockey

International Olympic Committee   **www.olympic.org**
The official site of the International Olympic Committee, with information on all Olympic sports

United States Curling Association (USA Curling)   **www.curlingrocks.net**
The official site of the U.S. governing body of curling

USA Hockey Inc.   **www.usahockey.com**
The official site of the U.S. governing body of ice hockey

World Curling Federation   **www.worldcurling.org**
The official site of the international governing body of curling

INDEX

COUNTRY ABBREVIATIONS

CAN — Canada
CZE — Czechoslovakia/
  Czech Republic
FIN — Finland
GER — Germany
RUS — Russia
SWE — Sweden
URS — Soviet Union
  (1922–1992)
USA — United States
  of America

Printed in the U.S.A. — CG